- Geography
- Government
- Economics

IDAHO HISTORY
Workbook for Kids

1

Ages 8 - 12

Social Studies Passages, Worksheets, Projects, & Activities

#mbcreations4education

Idaho History Workbook for Kids©
Copyright <<2024>> Megan Bell Smith
Cover and Illustrations ©[Megan Bell Smith] via Canva.com

Teachers are permitted to copy pages from this workbook for use with one class of students. Please do not distribute copies to other teachers, classes, or schools. The workbook and its contents may not be used for any commercial purposes.

Email questions to meganbsmithbooks@gmail.com

GET READY!

Teaching social studies is exciting, and this Idaho History Workbook for Kids will bring a new level of engagement to your 3rd, 4th, and 5th-grade students. Studying state history is crucial for upper elementary students as it helps them understand their local heritage, develop a sense of community, and connect historical events to their own lives.

Hear from Parents and Educators:
- "My daughter loved completing these social studies activities. I appreciated that it's not just worksheets, but also incorporates projects that are fun and engaging for a reluctant learner."
- "This resource was fun and easy to use. My 3rd and 4th-grade kids loved solving the mysteries."
- "I have really enjoyed using these planned-out pages to explore Idaho with my kiddo from our home. I have loved the project ideas and the worksheets."
- "This is the exact resource I was looking for to bring our old Idaho History textbooks to life. This workbook puts a fun and exciting twist on social studies lessons."

Topics included in Book 1:
1. Where in the World?
2. All About Idaho
3. Idaho Symbols
4. Idaho Counties
5. Famous Idahoans
6. Government
7. Economics

Topics included in Book 2:
1. Five Tribes of Idaho
2. Native American Culture
3. Lewis and Clark
4. Fur Trapping
5. Gold Rush
6. Oregon Trail
7. Settlements
8. Homesteading
9. Changes in Idaho
10. Transcontinental Railroad
11. Immigrants' Experiences

Recommendations:
- Spend two weeks of the school year discussing each topic. Invite students to present their finished projects to the class or share them with family members.
- Hire a paper supply store to add spiral binding to this workbook.

WHAT'S INSIDE

Topics:
1. Where in the World?
2. All About Idaho
3. Idaho Symbols
4. Idaho Counties
5. Famous Idahoans
6. Government
7. Economics

Each topic includes:
- Read All About It
- Practice Page
- Mystery Activity
- Assessments
- Answer Keys (in the back)

You'll also find a variety of projects throughout the book.

READ ALL ABOUT IT

Where in the World?

Name: _____

Introduction
We live in a vast universe made up of many planets. Map makers have divided places on Earth into many categories to help us make sense of our world. Read about them below!

Continents
A continent is a large body of land with ocean on the sides. There are seven continents in the world: Africa, Antarctica, Asia, Australia, Europe, North America, and South America. Each continent is home to unique species of plants and animals, as well as people from many cultures.

Oceans
There are five oceans in the world: the Arctic, Atlantic, Indian, Pacific, and Southern. Ocean water covers more than 70 percent of the Earth's surface and is home to much of Earth's wildlife.

Hemispheres
The equator is an imaginary line that circles the middle of the Earth. Map makers divide the planet into the northern and southern hemisphere using this line. Additionally, the Primed Meridian is an imaginary line that runs vertically between the north and south poles. This line splits the Earth into the eastern and western hemispheres.

Countries and States
Continents lie inside each hemisphere and are broken up even further into countries. A country is a territory of land that has its own government. Furthermore, countries are divided into states and cities where people live and form communities.

Discuss
- Why is the Earth organized in all of these different ways?
- Since many people follow apps on their cell phones, why is it important to learn about maps?

MB Creations

PRACTICE

Where in the World?

Name: _____

Directions: Answer the questions below. Use additional resources as needed.

1. What is the name of our planet? _____

2. What is our continent? _____

3. Which hemisphere do we live in? _____

4. What states border Idaho? (There are six!)

_____ _____ _____

_____ _____ _____

5. What is Idaho's capital city? _____

6. Fill in the cardinal directions on the compass rose:

7. Sometimes people think of a mnemonic (new-mon-ick) to remember cardinal directions. What phrase or words help you?

_____
_____
_____
_____
_____

MB Creations

PRACTICE

Where in the World?

Name:_____

Directions: Look at the list of places. Then, determine four different ways you could categorize them and write a label in each box. Finally, sort the places accordingly.

Places

Idaho	China	Pacific	Southern	Florida
Atlantic	Arctic	Africa	Asia	France
Canada	Ohio	Brazil	Australia	Texas

MB Creations

PROJECT

Where in the World?   Name: _____

Directions: Design your own island! Create locations that tell about your personality and interests. You could draw the land outline in the shape of a letter from your name or it could resemble an object that is important to you. Use the space below to get started.

Materials:

- Paper
- Colored Pencils
- Markers
- Crayons
- Ruler
- Black Sharpie
- Water Color Paints

These are suggestions. Use what you have available!

Things to Include:

- ☐ Your Name
- ☐ Map Title
- ☐ Compass Rose
- ☐ 6 Symbols
- ☐ Key or Legend (What do the symbols on your map mean?)
- ☐ 3 Land Features

Brainstorm/Sketch:

Plan your project before beginning. It's ok to make changes later!

MB Creations

ASSESSMENT
> Where in the World?

Name: _____

Directions: Write the corresponding letter of each place by its name.

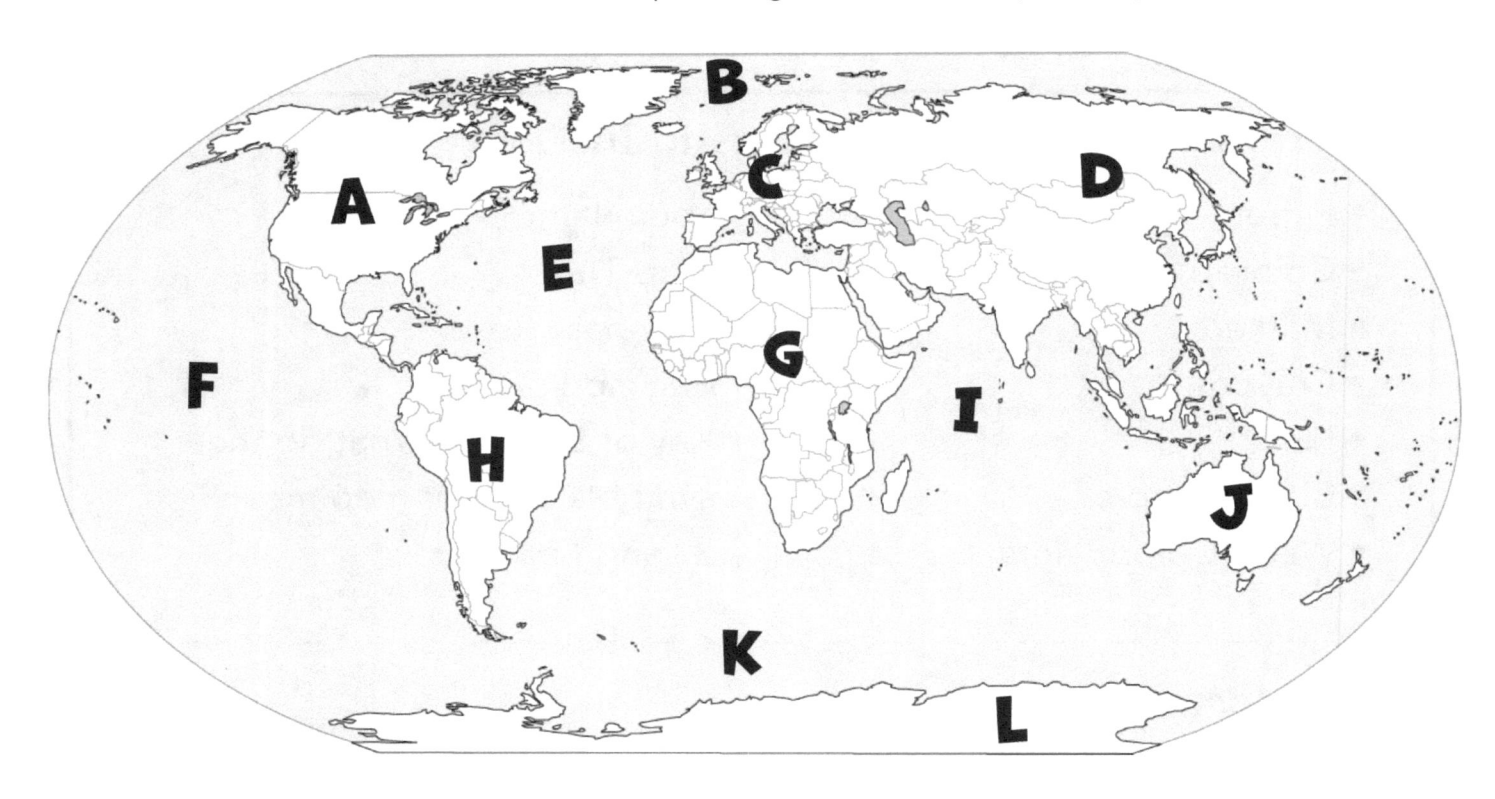

_____ South America   _____ Arctic

_____ Australia   _____ Atlantic

_____ Pacific   _____ Africa

_____ North America   _____ Southern

_____ Indian   _____ Asia

_____ Antarctica   _____ Europe

MB Creations

ASSESSMENT

>> Where in the World?

Name: _____

Directions: Compare and contrast two continents of your choice. Describe their locations using key terms from this lesson. Tell about their size, climates, plant and animal life, cultures, and other details you know.

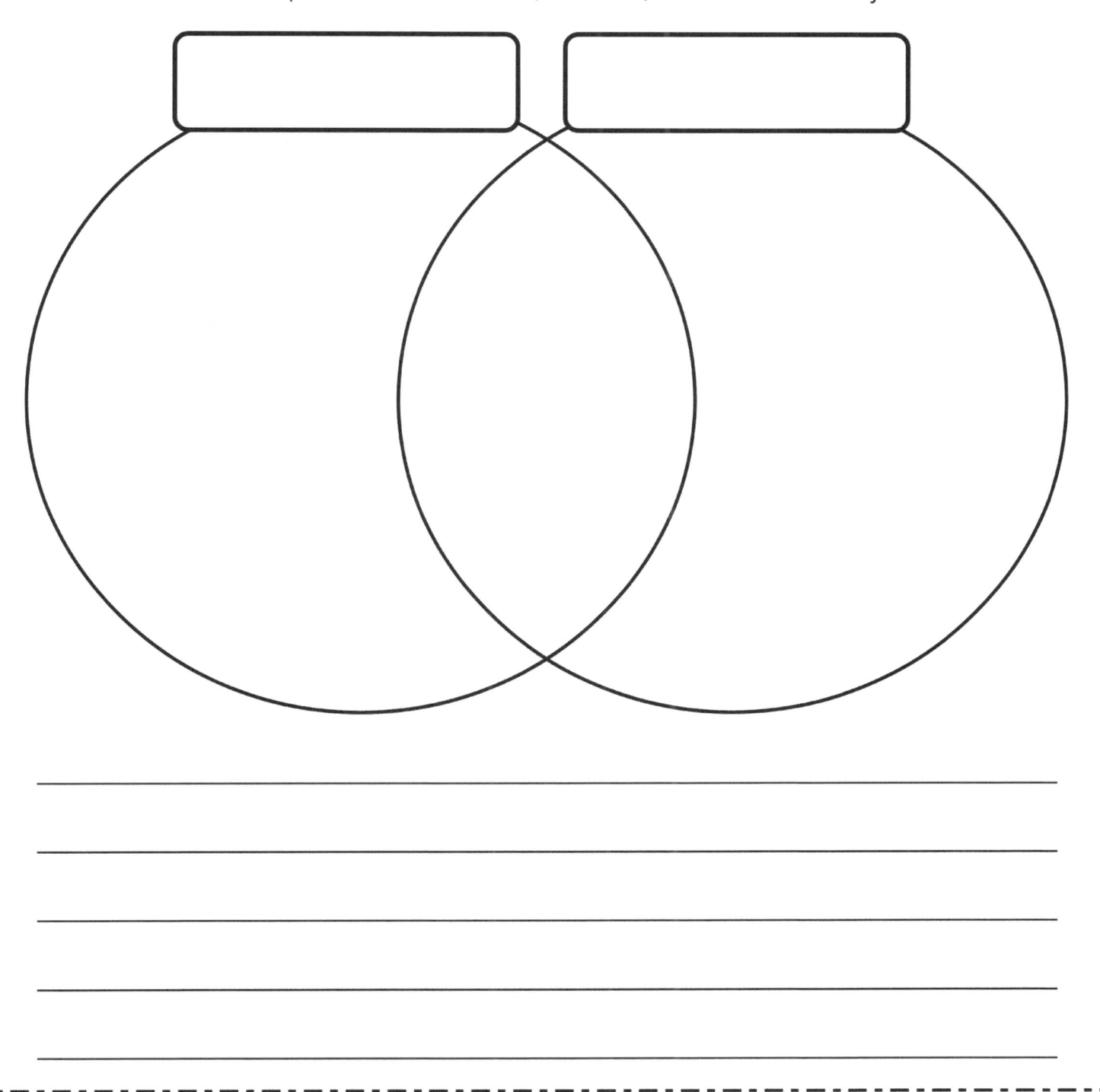

_____
_____
_____
_____
_____

MB Creations

MYSTERY

Where in the World?

Name:_____

Directions: Unscramble the letters to form words. Use the letters to discover the secret code below.

s e b i o	_ ★ _ _ _
f p c i a c i	✺ _ _ _ _ _ _
l y i t a	_ _ _ ▲ _
s h e h r e i m p e	_ _ _ _ _ ● _ _ _ _
o i h d a	_ ⬣ _ _ _
t a n c r a a c t i	_ _ _ _ ♥ _ _ _ _ _
m o g i w n y	_ _ _ _ ◆ _ _
g n a t s o i h w n	_ _ _ _ _ _ _ ⬟ _ _
h e r a t	■ _ _ _ _

CODE

_ _ _ _ _ _ _ _ _ _
⬟ ■ ★ ◆ ♥ ⬣ ✺ ● ▲

MB Creations

READ ALL ABOUT IT

Name:_____

All About Idaho

Natural Features

"Gem of the Mountains" is a perfect nickname for the state of Idaho because of its amazing natural features. Located in the Rocky Mountains, Idaho's lakes, rivers, wildflowers, and wild animals make it a beautiful place to explore. In addition, Idaho enjoys all four seasons throughout the year in its changing warm and cold climate in different months.

Seven Regions

Idaho is divided into seven regions, or areas that have commonalities. The North region is home to the deepest lakes in the state and touches the Canadian border. It is covered in thick forests and mountains. Below this area is the North Central region where rolling hills and prairies allow people to grow and harvest crops.

The Southwestern region is the most populated area of the state and is home to the capital - Boise. It features a variety of mountain ranges, valleys, and even deserts. The Central region has even more mountains and is a prime spot for hiking, camping, fishing, and skiing. People from all over the world visit Idaho to enjoy the great outdoors.

Crops also grow throughout the South Central region thanks to the Snake River. And right next-door in the Southeastern region, Idaho's famous potatoes grow in the rich soil. Finally, in the Eastern region, the Teton Mountains are home to many animals and make a breathtaking border against the state of Wyoming. With so many natural wonders, there is something for everyone in Idaho. Which region do you call home?

MB Creations

READ ALL ABOUT IT

Name: _____

All About Idaho

Places of Interest
Tourists visit Idaho to enjoy its natural beauties, relax, and explore. Have you been to any of these notable places?

Craters of the Moon National Monument
This area of land was created by volcanic eruptions many years ago. Lava left landforms that look like the surface of the moon. Visitors also travel through caves that are called lava tubes. These tubes used to be flowing with hot lava, but are now hollow.

Hell's Canyon
Along the border of Washington and Oregon, Hell's Canyon is the deepest river gorge in North America! The Snake River has carved out this gorge through the process of erosion.

City of Rocks
Pioneer travelers referred to this geological area as the City of Rocks because of its massive boulders and spires. It was an important landmark on the trail and today you can still see wagon ruts on the ground.

Shoshone Falls
This 212 foot waterfall is sometimes called "Niagara of the West." It is located in Twin Falls and has an amazing scenic overlook.

Quick Facts
- Highest Peak: Mount Borah - 12,662 feet
- Lowest Point: Lewiston - 738 feet
- Blackfoot, Idaho is the Potato Capital of the World

Discuss
- How do people use the natural resources in the region where you live?
- What regions have you visited in Idaho?

MB Creations

PRACTICE

All About Idaho   Name: _____

Directions: Use the readings and additional resources to answer the questions below.

1. Label each region. Then, list one city found in each region.

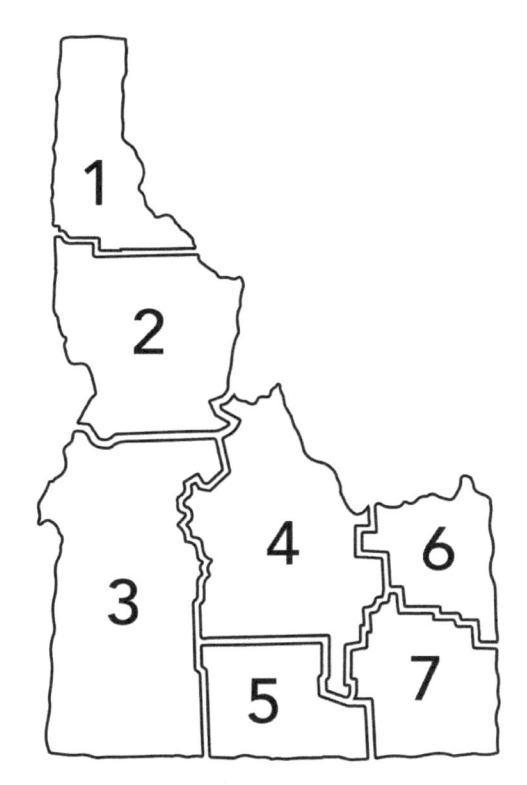

	Region:	City:
1		
2		
3		
4		
5		
6		
7		

2. Use a map and/or the Internet to match each of the following places to a region. (Not all regions will be used).

- Craters of the Moon ▶
- Yellowstone National Park ▶
- Potato Capital ▶
- Lake Coeur d'Alene ▶
- Boise Capitol Building ▶

- North
- North Central
- Southwest
- Central
- South Central
- Eastern
- Southeast

MB Creations

PROJECT

All About Idaho   Name: _____

Directions: Design a vacation brochure for Idaho. Include relevant facts, language of the discipline, images, maps, and sources. Consider planning a trip for a friend or family member who is visiting Idaho.

Materials:
- Paper (Construction paper or legal paper work great)
- Colored Pencils
- Markers
- Ruler
- Black Sharpie
- Magazines or printed pictures

These are suggestions. Use what you have available!

Things to Include:
- ☐ Your name
- ☐ Brochure title
- ☐ 3 cities
- ☐ 1 thing to do in each place
- ☐ Distance between cities
- ☐ _____
- ☐ _____

Brainstorm/Sketch:

Plan your project before beginning. It's ok to make changes later!

MB Creations

ASSESSMENT

All About Idaho

Name: _____

Directions: Cut on the dashed lines and match the clues to each region of Idaho.

North

North Central

Southwest

Central

Eastern

South Central

Southeast

- Home to Idaho's first capital (before it changed)
- Has rolling hills and prairies

- Includes a small part of Yellowstone National Park

- Popular place for tourists to ski, camp, and fish
- Major cities are Salmon & Stanley

- Potato capital of the world
- Has Lava Hot Springs

- Touches Canada
- Has lakes, forests, and mountains

- Craters of the Moon
- Shoshone Falls

- Home to Idaho's current capital city
- Has mountains, deserts, and valleys

MB Creations

ASSESSMENT

All About Idaho

Name: _____

Directions: Imagine you are visiting Idaho for the first time. Write a letter to a friend or family member who has never been here. (You can make up an imaginary name if needed). Tell them about some of the following:

☐ Landforms/Natural Features ☐ Cities ☐ Animals ☐ Notable Places

_____
_____
_____
_____
_____
_____
_____
_____
_____
_____
_____
_____

MB Creations

MYSTERY

All About Idaho

Name:_____

Directions: Complete the crossword puzzle and use the shapes to uncover the code.

Across
2. Number of regions in Idaho
5. Niagara of the West
7. Massive boulders and spires that became a landmark on the Oregon Trail
8. Lowest point in Idaho

Down
1. Area of land created by ancient volcanic eruptions
3. Idaho's Nickname
4. Potato Capital of the World
6. Highest Peak in Idaho

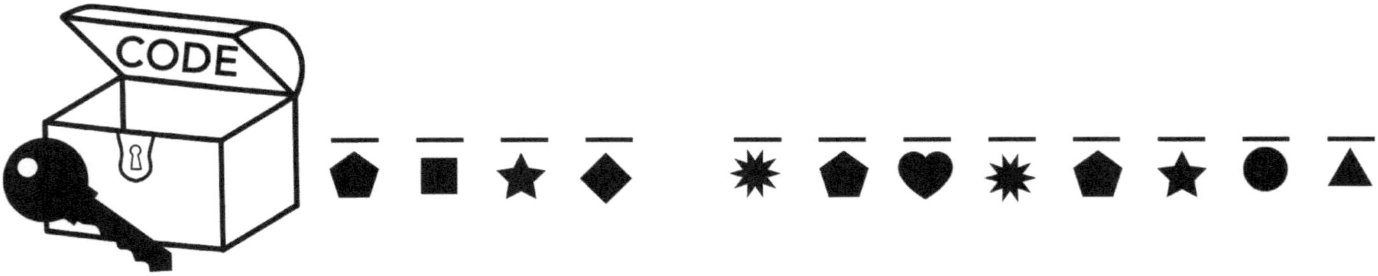

CODE

MB Creations

READ ALL ABOUT IT

Name:_____

Idaho Symbols

What is a symbol?

A state symbol is something unique and important to a specific place. Recognizing symbols helps people show pride for their state and its amazing features. Perhaps your school has a mascot. When students show pride about the mascot, they can feel more unified. Learning about state symbols is fun! Idaho has many symbols; here are just a few.

Amphibian: Giant Salamander	Bird: Mountain Bluebird	Dance: Square Dance	Fish: Cutthroat Trout
Flower: Syringa	Fossil: Hagerman Horse	Fruit: Huckleberry	Gem: Idaho Star Garnet
Horse: Appaloosa	Insect: Monarch Butterfly	Raptor: Peregrine Falcon	Tree: Western White Pine

Discuss
- If you were going to add another symbol to the state, what would you choose?

MB Creations

PRACTICE

Idaho Symbols   Name: _____

Directions: Find some of Idaho's symbols in the word search below.

```
R V A P G B E S A L A M A N D E R M
H U C K L E B E R R Y C T W W N R F
W H A G E R M A N H O R S E E Q S C
H M M S P E R E G R I N E K E P Y M
I O Y Q I T V M Z S R Q W L G M R U
T N W U Q E Z B L U E B I R D O I H
E A K A A F A Q J W Z E N Y N C N X
P R K R T R O U T Z C P L B G J G C
I C R E B C B M S E V W V I F W A W
N H I L G N F T P L H V Q K W K T M
E S S T A R G A R N E T G G Q G F Z
C E N A D X A P P A L O O S A N Z Q
```

Find the following words in the puzzle.
Words are hidden → ↓ and ↘.

APPALOOSA	PEREGRINE	TROUT
BLUEBIRD	SALAMANDER	WHITE PINE
HAGERMAN HORSE	SQUARE	
HUCKLEBERRY	STAR GARNET	
MONARCH	SYRINGA	

Extension: Some of the symbol names were shortened to fit in the puzzle. Circle the symbols in the word list that have been shortened from their full names.

MB Creations

GAME

Idaho Symbols

Name: _____

Directions: Play a memory game! Begin by cutting apart the cards. Turn over the cards and try to match each name to the correct symbol.

State Amphibian	State Bird	State Dance
State Fish	State Flower	State Fossil
State Fruit	State Gem	State Horse
State Insect	State Raptor	State Tree

MB Creations

GAME

Idaho Symbols

Name: _____

Directions: Play a memory game! Begin by drawing pictures of the symbols. Then, cut and turn over the cards. Try to match each name to the correct symbol.

Syringa	Mountain Bluebird	Idaho Star Garnet
Giant Salamander	Hagerman Horse	Peregrine Falcon
Appaloosa	Huckleberry	Western White Pine
Square Dance	Cutthroat Trout	Monarch Butterfly

MB Creations

PROJECT

Idaho Symbols   Name: _____

Directions: Design bumper stickers for cars in Idaho! Choose at least one symbol to use in each design. You can add fun phrases and words that repesent Idaho, too.

Materials:
- Paper
- Scissors
- Colored Pencils
- Markers
- Crayons
- Black Sharpie

These are suggestions. Use what you have available!

Things to Include on Each Sticker:
- ☐ Your Name (write on the back)
- ☐ At least one symbol
- ☐ Color
- ☐ A Word/Phrase

Brainstorm/Sketch:

Plan your project before beginning. It's ok to make changes later!

MB Creations

ASSESSMENT

Idaho Symbols

Name:_____

Directions: Write as many Idaho symbols on the bingo board below. Can you get...

☐ three across?   ☐ four down?   ☐ all four corners?   ☐ the entire board?

Flower:	Bird:	Gem:
Amphibian:	Fossil:	Raptor:
Horse:	Fruit:	Tree:
Dance:	Fish:	Insect:

MB Creations

ASSESSMENT

Idaho Symbols

Name: _____

Directions: Imagine the governor calls your principal and asks for students to create another symbol for Idaho. Draw a picture of what you would choose and describe why this symbol is important in our state.

_____

_____

_____

_____

_____

_____

MB Creations

MYSTERY

Idaho Symbols

Name: _____

Write the symbols for our state. Then, list in order from Z to A.
Take the first letter of each name and fill in the code to win the game!

- Bird: _____

- Dance: _____

- Fish: _____

- Flower: _____

- Fossil: _____

- Fruit: _____

- Gem: _____

- Horse: _____

- Insect: _____

- Tree: _____

CODE

_ _ _ _ _ _ _ _ _ _

MB Creations

READ ALL ABOUT IT

Name: _____

Idaho's Counties

What is a county?

Idaho has a total of forty-four counties across the state. A county is a small region of land that has cities and towns within its borders. The people within each county vote on an elected official to make decisions for their area.

License Plates

Most license plates in the state begin with a number and letter to represent the county in which you live. It can be fun to pay attention to license plates as you drive down the highway if you know the counties. Review the list below!

1A **Ada** (Boise)	4C **Cassia** (Burley)	3L **Lewis** (Nez Perce)
2A **Adams** (Council)	5C **Clark** (Dubois)	4L **Lincoln** (Shoshone)
1B **Bannock** (Pocatello)	6C **Clearwater** (Orofino)	1M **Madison** (Rexburg)
2B **Bear Lake** (Paris)	7C **Custer** (Challis)	2M **Minidoka** (Rupert)
3B **Benewah** (St. Maries)	E **Elmore** (Mountain Home)	N **Nez Perce** (Lewiston)
4B **Bingham** (Blackfoot)	1F **Franklin** (Preston)	1O **Oneida** (Malad City)
5B **Blaine** (Hailey)	2F **Fremont** (St. Anthony)	2O **Owyhee** (Murphy)
6B **Boise** (Idaho City)	1G **Gem** (Emmett)	1P **Payette** (Payette)
7B **Bonner** (Sandpoint)	2G **Gooding** (Gooding)	2P **Power** (American Falls)
8B **Bonneville** (Idaho Falls)	I **Idaho** (Grangeville)	S **Shoshone** (Wallace)
9B **Boundary** (Bonners Ferry)	1J **Jefferson** (Rigby)	1T **Teton** (Driggs)
10B **Butte** (Arco)	2J **Jerome** (Jerome)	2T **Twin Falls** (Twin Falls)
1C **Camas** (Fairfield)	K **Kootenai** (Coeur d'Alene)	V **Valley** (Cascade)
2C **Canyon** (Caldwell)	1L **Latah** (Moscow)	W **Washington** (Weiser)
3C **Caribou** (Soda Springs)	2L **Lemhi** (Salmon)	

Discuss

- Based on where you live, what could your license plate begin with?
- How are counties, states, and cities different? How are they related?

MB Creations

PRACTICE

Idaho's Counties

Name: _____

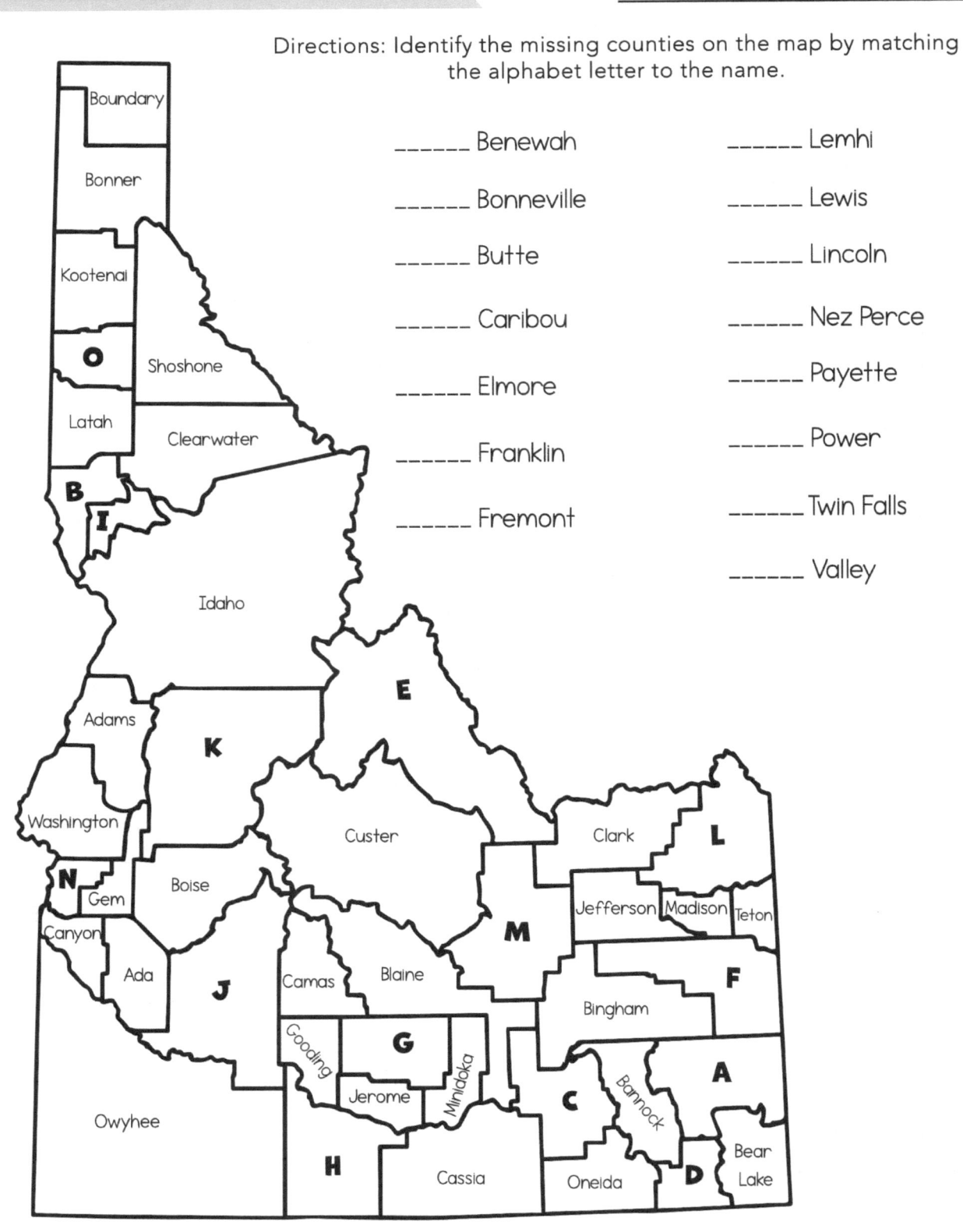

Directions: Identify the missing counties on the map by matching the alphabet letter to the name.

_____ Benewah   _____ Lemhi

_____ Bonneville   _____ Lewis

_____ Butte   _____ Lincoln

_____ Caribou   _____ Nez Perce

_____ Elmore   _____ Payette

_____ Franklin   _____ Power

_____ Fremont   _____ Twin Falls

_____ Valley

MB Creations

PROJECT

Idaho's Counties

Name: _____

Directions: Design a license plate specific to a single county. Think of a way to incorporate images or designs that represent facts about the county. Also refer to your "Read All About It" page to find the county's beginning letters. Can you also think of a creative phrase to use for the final letters on your plate? (Ex. 1A SMILE)

Materials:
- Paper or the License Plate Template
- Colored Pencils
- Markers
- Crayons
- Black Sharpie

These are suggestions. Use what you have available!

Things to Include:
- ☐ Your Name
- ☐ County Number/Beginning Letter
- ☐ Additional Letters/Numbers
- ☐ A symbol or image that represents something special about the county

Brainstorm/Sketch:

Plan your project before beginning. It's ok to make changes later!

MB Creations

PROJECT

Idaho's Counties

Name: _____

Directions: Design a license plate specific to a single county.

MB Creations

ASSESSMENT

Idaho's Counties

Name: _____

Directions: Choose three counties. Label them on the map, and tell something about each one. Then, answer the multiple-choice questions.

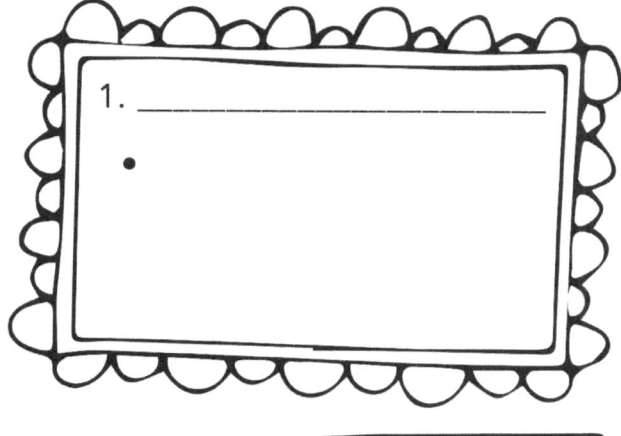

1. _____
   •

2. _____
   •

3. _____
   •

4. How are leaders in a county chosen?
   A) they campaign
   B) they are elected
   C) the people vote for them
   D) all of the above

5. What are parts of a county?
   A) states and countries
   B) towns and cities
   C) cities and states
   D) countries and territories

MB Creations

ASSESSMENT

>> Idaho's Counties

Name:_____

Directions: Use knowledge from your research to answer the questions below.

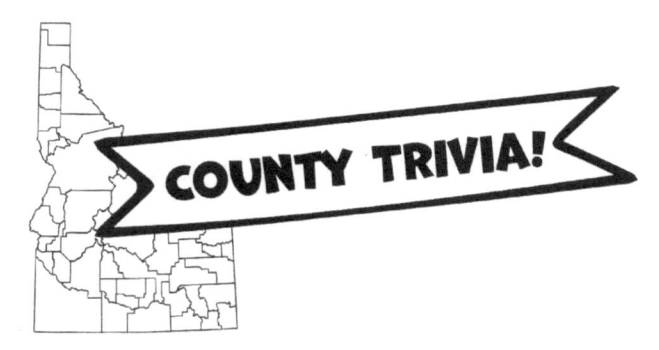

COUNTY TRIVIA!

1. Which of the following counties was the first to be organized?

    A) Boise
    B) Owyhee
    C) Gooding
    D) Lewis

2. How many counties were already part of the Idaho Territory when Idaho became a state in 1890?

    A) 18
    B) 44
    C) 3
    D) 28

3. What is Idaho's largest county by size (square miles)?

    A) Camas
    B) Elmore
    C) Bingham
    D) Idaho

4. What is Idaho's smallest county by size (square miles)?

    A) Payette
    B) Cassia
    C) Teton
    D) Washington

5. What is Idaho's most populated county?

    A) Gem
    B) Ada
    C) Kootenai
    D) Boundary

6. What is Idaho's least populated county?

    A) Madison
    B) Lincoln
    C) Power
    D) Clark

7. In which county is the capital city located?

    A) Canyon
    B) Jerome
    C) Boise
    D) Ada

MB Creations

MYSTERY

44 Counties 1A

Name:_____

Directions: Many of Idaho's counties are listed below. However, one additional county from another state is listed. Which one doesn't belong?

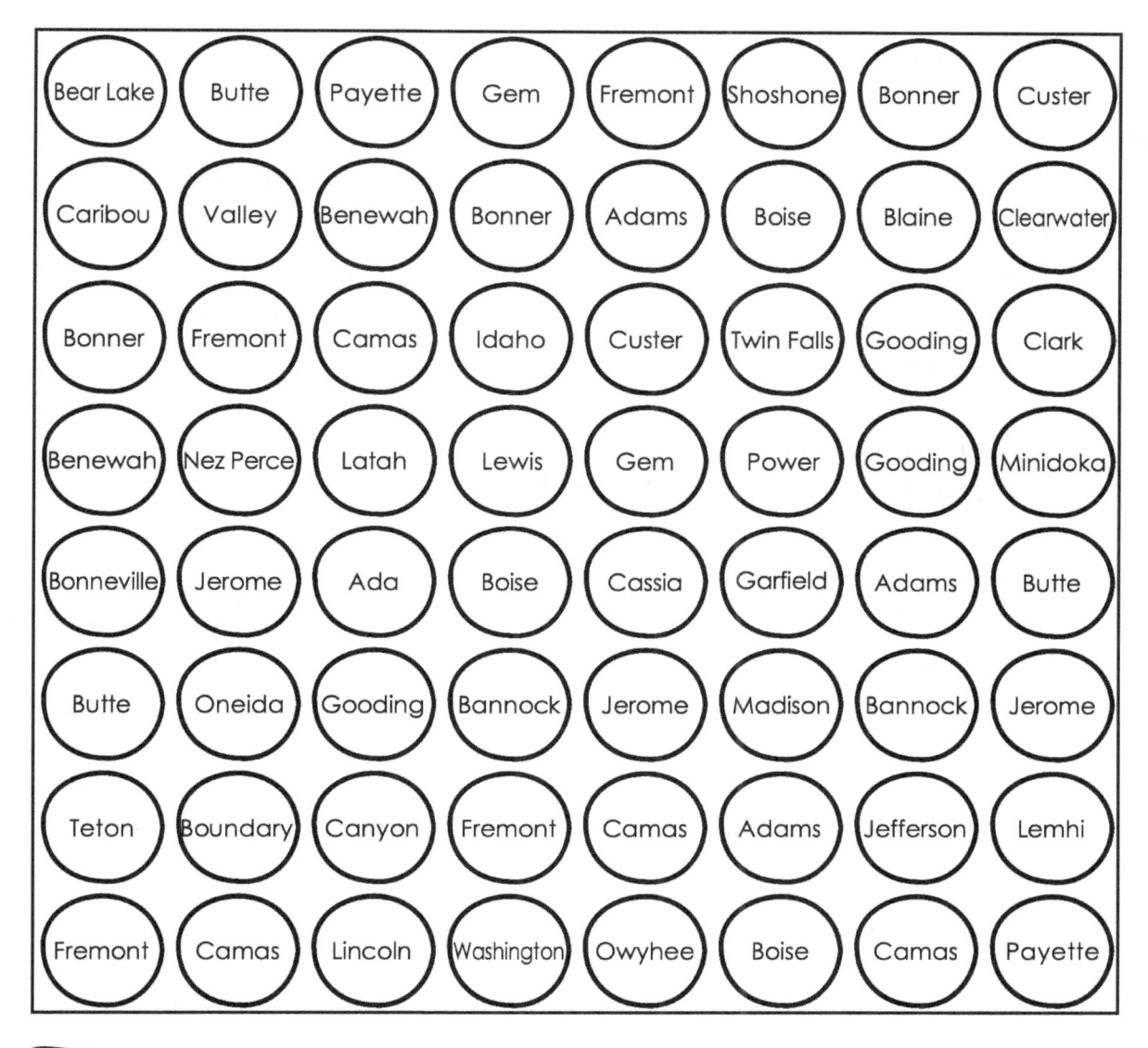

Bear Lake	Butte	Payette	Gem	Fremont	Shoshone	Bonner	Custer
Caribou	Valley	Benewah	Bonner	Adams	Boise	Blaine	Clearwater
Bonner	Fremont	Camas	Idaho	Custer	Twin Falls	Gooding	Clark
Benewah	Nez Perce	Latah	Lewis	Gem	Power	Gooding	Minidoka
Bonneville	Jerome	Ada	Boise	Cassia	Garfield	Adams	Butte
Butte	Oneida	Gooding	Bannock	Jerome	Madison	Bannock	Jerome
Teton	Boundary	Canyon	Fremont	Camas	Adams	Jefferson	Lemhi
Fremont	Camas	Lincoln	Washington	Owyhee	Boise	Camas	Payette

CODE

Find the dot that's out of place.
Write it's name and win the race!

MB Creations

READ ALL ABOUT IT

Name: _____

Famous Idahoans

People born in Idaho, as well as those who have moved there later in life, have had a great influence on the world. Read about a few individuals whose unique impact has touched the lives of thousands of Americans and beyond.

Gutzon Borglum (1867 - 1941)

Born in Bear Lake, Idaho, Gutzon Borglum is best known for sculpting the faces of Mount Rushmore. This is a massive memorial of George Washington, Thomas Jefferson, Theodore Roosevelt and Abraham Lincoln. He carved it into the side of a mountain in South Dakota. His 14 years of work were initially left unfinished when he passed away, but later completed by his son.

Philo T. Farnsworth (1906 - 1971)

Philo Taylor Farnsworth moved to Rigby, Idaho when he was twelve years old and is known as a founder of television. He was fascinated with technology and wanted to be an inventor. His high school chemistry teacher helped tutor him as he worked on his idea of the television. He completed his first prototype at the age of twenty-one.

Joe Albertson (1906 - 1993)

Joseph Albertson grew up in Caldwell, Idaho, and is the founder of the Albertson's grocery store chain. Today, these grocery stores dot the entire United States. He gained experience in this industry working for and supervising Safeway stores. When he opened his first store in Boise, his goal was to offer quality, good value, and excellent service. During World War II, he filled his shelves with additional items like household goods and beauty products. This allowed people to stop at only one place to shop and became a popular system in many stores.

Discuss
- What do these three people have in common?
- What other Idahoans do you know about who have influenced America?

MB Creations

PRACTICE

Famous Idahoans

Name: _____

Directions: Draw a picture and write about each of the famous Idahoans described on the "Read All About It" page.

MB Creations

PROJECT

Famous Idahoans   Name: _____

Directions: Create a "Who Am I?" poster with clues and artwork about a famous Idahoan.
1. Choose a person to study. Look at the suggestions for inspiration.
2. Write 5 to 10 clues on one piece of paper.
3. Write your person's full name on a second piece of paper and staple it underneath the clues.
4. Create artwork of your person. Consider tearing paper as shown in the example.
5. Attach your artwork to your clues.

Materials:

- Construction Paper
- Paper for Clues
- Colored Pencils
- Markers

These are suggestions. Use what you have available!

Things to Include:

- ☐ Your Name
- ☐ 5 to 10 clues
- ☐ Your Person's Full Name
- ☐ Artwork of Your Person

Brainstorm/Sketch:

Plan your project before beginning. It's ok to make changes later!

MB Creations

PROJECT

Famous Idahoans   Name: _____

Who Am I? - Suggestions to Study:

*Note - Not all of the people on this list were born in Idaho, but they lived in or impacted Idaho at some point in their lives.

Joe	Albertson		Juanita Uberaga	Hormaechea
Cecil	Andrus		Michael	Jordan
Jesse A.	Applegate		Chief	Joseph
John Jacob	Astor		Noah	Kellogg
Vernon	Baker		Jason	Lee
Wilbur	Bassett		Robert	Limbert
James Pierson	Beckwourth		Hai	Ly
Polly	Bemis		Ira	Perrine
Benjamin	Bonneville		Elias	Pierce
Cherie	Buckner-Webb		Edward	Pulaski
Joseph	Cataldo		Statira E Gibbons	Robinson
Frank	Church		Sacajawea	
Don E.	Crabtree		George L	Shoup
William	Craig		J. R.	Simplot
Pierre Jean	De Smet		Robert E	Smylie
Emma Smith	DeVoe		Henry or Eliza	Spalding
Abigail Scott	Duniway		Moses	Splawn
Larry	Echohawk		Robert or Craig	Strahorn
Philo T.	Farnsworth		David	Thompson
Mary Hallock	Foote		Chief	Timothy
Gretchen Kunigk	Fraser		Amy	Trice
John C.	Fremont		Jesus	Urquides
Henry	Fujii		William	Wallace
George	Grigsby		Marcus or Narcissa	Whitman
George	Grimes		Kitty	Wilkins
Gene	Harris		Norman B	Willey
John	Healy		Nathaniel	Wyeth
Andrew	Henry		Brigham	Young

MB Creations

PROJECT

Famous Idahoans   Name:_____

Who Am I?

Paper-Tearing Art

Tips:

- Sketch the person first
- Tear a pile of paper
- Shuffle the paper pieces around to make them fit and then glue down

Clues

MB Creations

ASSESSMENT

Famous Idahoans

Name: _____

Directions: Show what you have learned about Idahoans by answering the questions below.

1. Match the famous Idahoans to one of their accomplishments.

   Gutzon Borglum ▶   ◀ Founded a grocery-store that has grown into a large chain today

   J.R. Simplot ▶   ◀ Invented the television

   Phil T. Farnsworth ▶   ◀ Sculpted presidents' faces on Mount Rushmore

   Joe Albertson ▶   ◀ Supplied McDonalds with the first frozen french fries from potatoes he grew in Idaho

2. Write about another Idahoan you studied. What impact did they have on this state? (This may be someone you read about in your textbook, researched for your "Who Am I?" project, or learned about from a peer's project.)

   _____
   _____
   _____
   _____
   _____
   _____
   _____

MB Creations

ASSESSMENT

» Famous Idahoans

Name:_____

Directions: Choose a person from this list or write your own (person who impacted Idaho). Then, answer the questions from that person's perspective.

Person:
- ☐ Chief Joseph
- ☐ Elias Pierce
- ☐ Statira Robinson
- ☐ Joe Albertson
- ☐ _____

1. How do you think your person would feel about the building of the Transcontinental Railroad? Why?

2. How do you think your person would feel about giving women the right to vote (suffrage)? Why?

3. How do you think your person would feel about helping the United States military during World War II? Why?

MB Creations

MYSTERY

Famous Idahoans

Name: _____

Directions: Decipher the rebus puzzles below by writing the first and last names of people who impacted Idaho. Then, use one of the names to decipher the code.

🔘p=w+🐏r=i 🌊-ve+🔔-be+a+🍚-ri pill ram wave bell rice	j+👞-sh shoe a+💡-bu+e+🎯-da+☀️u=o bulb dart sun
⬆️-u+🎩-at+i+🔒-ck up hat lock 🚗c=f+🗽y=s🐺-lf+🎯-da+h car ny wolf dart	c+👔t=h+f 🌹r=j+⬆️-u+h tie rose up
j+🐏-am ram 📼-vh+i+👨-an+🔌-ug+🐮x=t vhs man plug ox	🔘i=o+y pill 🔔-ll+m+⛷-sk+🚌-bu bell ski bus

CODE

To unlock the code, focus only on the last Fill in the letters and try to work fast.

__ __ __ __ __ __ __ __

MB Creations

READ ALL ABOUT IT

Name: _____

Government

What is Government?
Citizens of Idaho are required to follow rules and laws, and in return they are granted rights and responsibilities. The goal of these laws are to keep people safe and make our towns and cities comfortable places to live. This system is called government and it is the way in which our nation and states are ruled. There are multiple levels of government - starting with the national government at the top, followed by state and tribal rule underneath, and then succeeded by city and county governments.

Three Branches
Our government is divided into three branches to distribute control and responsibilities more evenly. This system of checks and balances keep a single branch from gaining too much power. The legislative branch makes laws and decisions for the people. At a national level, the legislative branch consists of Congress - the Senate and the House of Representatives. The executive branch caries out the laws and is run by the President of the United States. Finally, the judicial branch enforces the laws and is made up of our court system. They make sure laws do not go against the Constitution and make decisions about people who do not abide by the laws.

Tribal Governments
The five federally-recognized Native American tribes in Idaho also have their own forms of government. Tribal governments work to protect the people in their tribe and persevere natural resources. They have power over their reservations, but still have to abide by the laws established through the national government. Similar to national and state governments, tribal governments also utilize three branches of power.

Discuss
- In your opinion, which branch of government is most important? Why?
- If you were to write a constitution for your classroom, what might you include?

MB Creations

PRACTICE

Government

Name: _____

Directions: Use your knowledge and information from the reading to answer the questions below.

1. Write the name of each type of government in order of rank and power. Which government is at the top (and has overarching rule)?

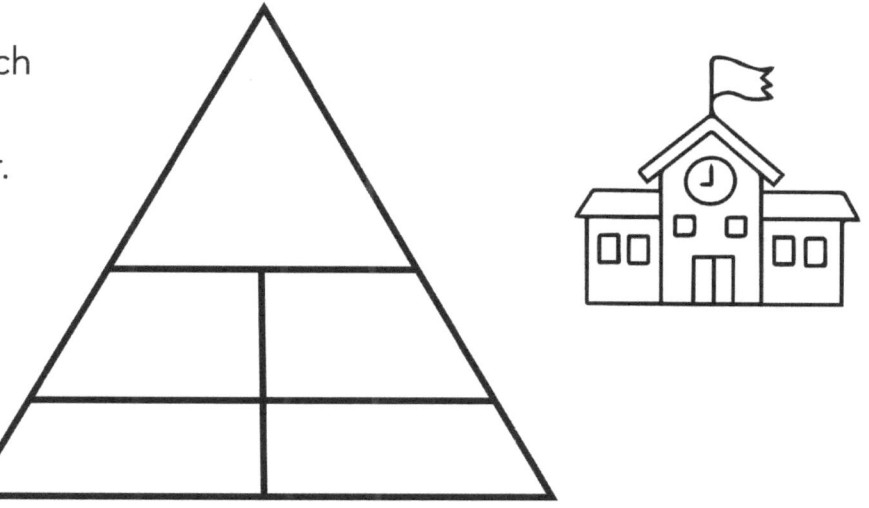

2. What are the three branches of national government? List one power of each branch. (What do they do?)

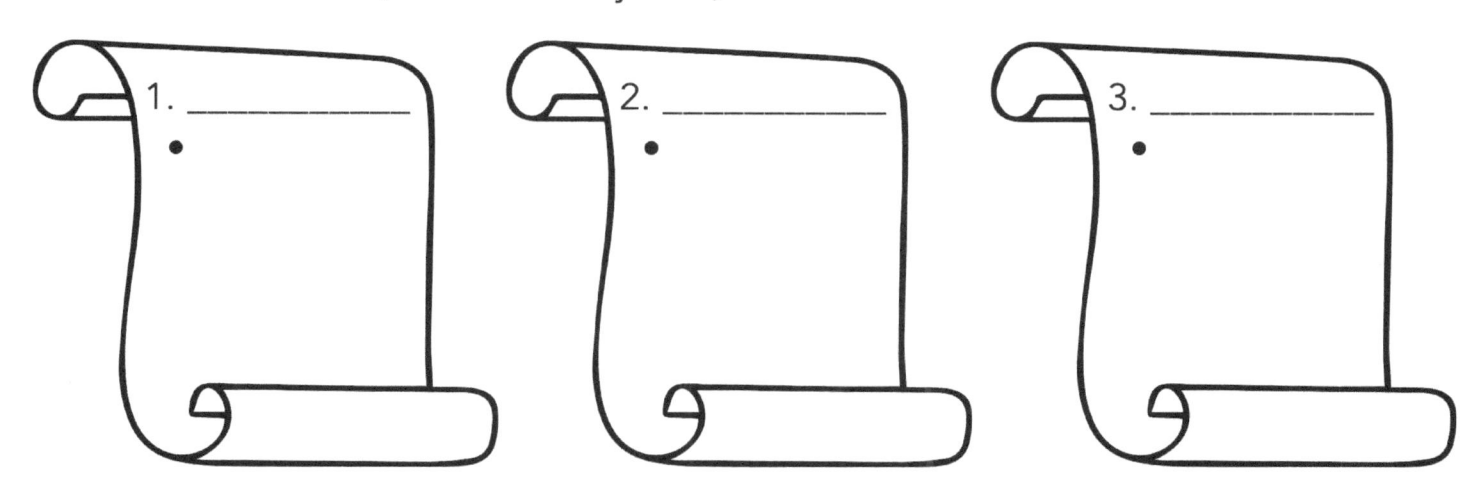

1. _____
-

2. _____
-

3. _____
-

3. Why is our government organized into three different branches?

_____

_____

_____

MB Creations

SIMULATION

Government   Name: _____

CREATE A GOVERNMENT

When the early leaders of the United States wrote the Constitution, they evaluated what rights and laws were most important. Now is your chance to try setting up your own government! You have 20 tokens to spend on elements that make up our current government. Each time you color in a white box, cross off one token. Choose how to spend your tokens wisely by thinking of which powers and responsibilities are most important to you.

Tokens: ① ② ③ ④ ⑤ ⑥ ⑦ ⑧ ⑨ ⑩ ⑪ ⑫ ⑬ ⑭ ⑮ ⑯ ⑰ ⑱ ⑲ ⑳

Legislative Branch:

- ☐ Includes a House of Representatives (number of congressmen based on population)
- ☐ Includes a Senate (two senators from each state)
- ☐☐ Approve people appointed by the president to serve in government positions
- ☐☐ Distribute government money and tax the people
- ☐☐ Power to declare war
- ☐☐☐ Write your own: _____

Executive Branch:

- ☐☐ Run by a President who is elected by the people every four years
- ☐ Can propose new laws
- ☐☐ Can veto laws
- ☐ Chooses people to serve in government positions
- ☐ Appoints judges to serve in federal courts
- ☐☐☐ Write your own: _____

Judicial Branch:

- ☐ Includes 9 justices in the Supreme Court
- ☐☐ Can determine if Congress and/or the president are following the constitution or not
- ☐☐ Ensures the government and citizens follow the law
- ☐ Resolves conflicts brought to the courts by people, states, and branches of government
- ☐☐☐ Write your own: _____

MB Creations

PROJECT

Government   Name: _____

Directions: Design your own game to teach students about the three branches of government. You may want to follow the pattern of another game you have played.

Materials:
- Paper
- Colored Pencils
- Markers
- Crayons
- Scissors
- Ruler
- Game Pieces/Dice
- Black Sharpie

These are suggestions. Use what you have available!

Things to Include:
- [ ] Your name
- [ ] Instructions on how to play
- [ ] Game board, cards, or pieces
- [ ] Questions that relate to this topic

Brainstorm/Sketch:

Plan your project before beginning. It's ok to make changes later!

Inspiration from Other Games:
- Bingo
- Candy Land
- Chutes and Ladders
- Guess Who
- Memory
- Monopoly
- Pictionary/Charades
- Sorry
- Trivia Games
- Uno

MB Creations

ASSESSMENT

Government

Name:_____

1. Who runs each branch of government at the national level in the United States?

Legislative Branch:	Executive Branch:	Judicial Branch:

2. True or False...

_____ A tribal government overrules the federal government.

_____ State and city governments utilize a system of checks and balances by dividing up responsibilities similar to the federal government.

_____ The executive branch makes laws for the people based on the Constitution.

_____ The president decides how many senators from each state can join Congress.

_____ The legislative branch taxes the people and manages government funds.

3. If you were to write a constitution for your school or classroom, what rights and laws would you include? Why?

_____
_____
_____
_____
_____
_____
_____

MB Creations

MYSTERY

Name:_____

Directions: Match each word to the correct branch of government.

President	Court	Interprets Laws	Interprets Laws	Senate	President	Senate	Senate
Vice President	Court	Judge	Chief Justice	Interprets Laws	Chief Justice	Congress	Senate
Chief Justice	Judge	Court	Judge	Court	Judge	President	House of R
House of R	Vice President	House of R	President	Chief Justice	Court	Senate	Interprets Laws
Makes Laws	Makes Laws	House of R	Chief Justice	Chief Justice	Interprets Laws	Chief Justice	Carries Out Laws
Carries Out Laws	Judge	Makes Laws	President	Vice President	Judge	Carries Out Laws	House of R

Legislative Branch:

Executive Branch:

Judicial Branch:

CODE

To unlock this code, use three numbers in line.
Count the dots in each branch and it will open just fine.

___ ___ ___

MB Creations

READ ALL ABOUT IT

Name:_____

Economics

Introduction

Every time you go to the store, you are witnessing economics all around you! Think about a grocery store. Someone helped grow the vegetables you see on the shelves or helped process the meat in the refrigerated section. Then, another person transported those goods from farms and factories to the store. Still, other people helped stock the shelves and run the operational side of the business. Isn't it great that when you arrive on the scene, you can pick out your favorite foods, purchase them, and take them home with such ease?

Goods and Services

Economics is the study of production, distribution, and use of goods and services. Unlike foods at the grocery store, a service is something you receive that is not tangible. Examples include getting your haircut, hiring a cleaning company, and medical consulting. Many careers you might consider in the future deal with providing services to other people.

Supply and Demand

Sometimes certain goods run out or are difficult to find. This is known as scarcity. It is the opposite of abundance. During the Covid Pandemic, some goods were not available to consumers (customers buying the products), for a short time. If the supply of a product is low, the demand typically increases.

Think about it this way... If your teacher brought one cookie to class and set it on the front table, most students would be excited to eat the cookie! At this time, cookies are very scarce in the classroom - there is only one! So, the demand for that cookie skyrockets. As a result, your teacher may offer the cookie at a high price. For example, any student who wants to stay inside from recess for a week and organize the bookshelves could get the cookie. In the real market, when supply is low, and demand is high, prices increase. Keeping the economy balanced can be a difficult task!

Discuss
- When do you see the process of economics in your own life?
- If you were making a list, what other words fit in the category of economics?

MB Creations

PRACTICE

Economics Name: _____

Directions: Use information from the reading and your own knowledge to answer the questions.

List 5 Goods:
- _____
- _____
- _____
- _____
- _____

List 5 Services:
- _____
- _____
- _____
- _____
- _____

Imagine you are talking to a friend about this class. Tell them something you know about each of these terms:

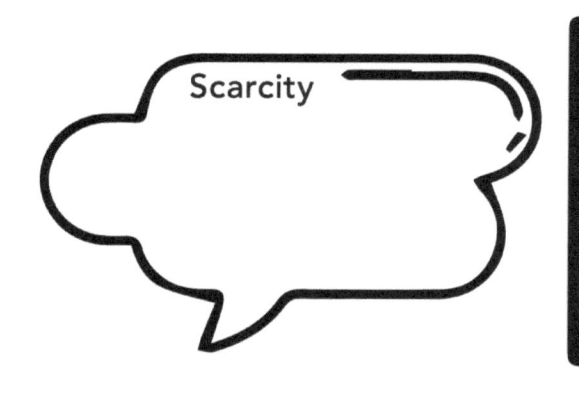

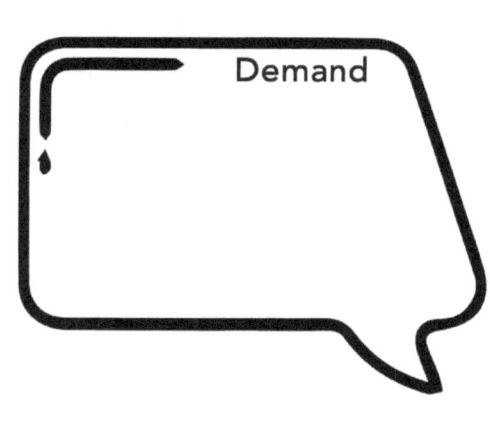

Scarcity

Supply

Demand

Draw a picture of a good you can buy at a store or restaurant:	Make a list of items used to make this good (Example: Sandwich - needs bread)	Choose an item from the list. Pretend it has just become scarce.	What happens to supply? What happens to the price?

MB Creations

ASSESSMENT

Economics

Name: _____

Directions: Answer the questions below.

1. Why is learning about economics important?

   _____
   _____
   _____
   _____

2. Look at the list below. Circle at least two items. Describe patterns you may see with supply and demand of each item.

   - Pumpkins in the month of November
   - Cell phone sales for Model 8 following the release of the new Model 9
   - Cupcake sales at the grocery store bakery if a new cupcake shop opens next door
   - Roses in the month of February
   - Gas prices during summer break when school is out of session

   _____
   _____
   _____
   _____
   _____
   _____

MB Creations

MYSTERY

Economics

Name: _____

Directions: Cut apart the puzzle pieces.
Connect the matching sides.

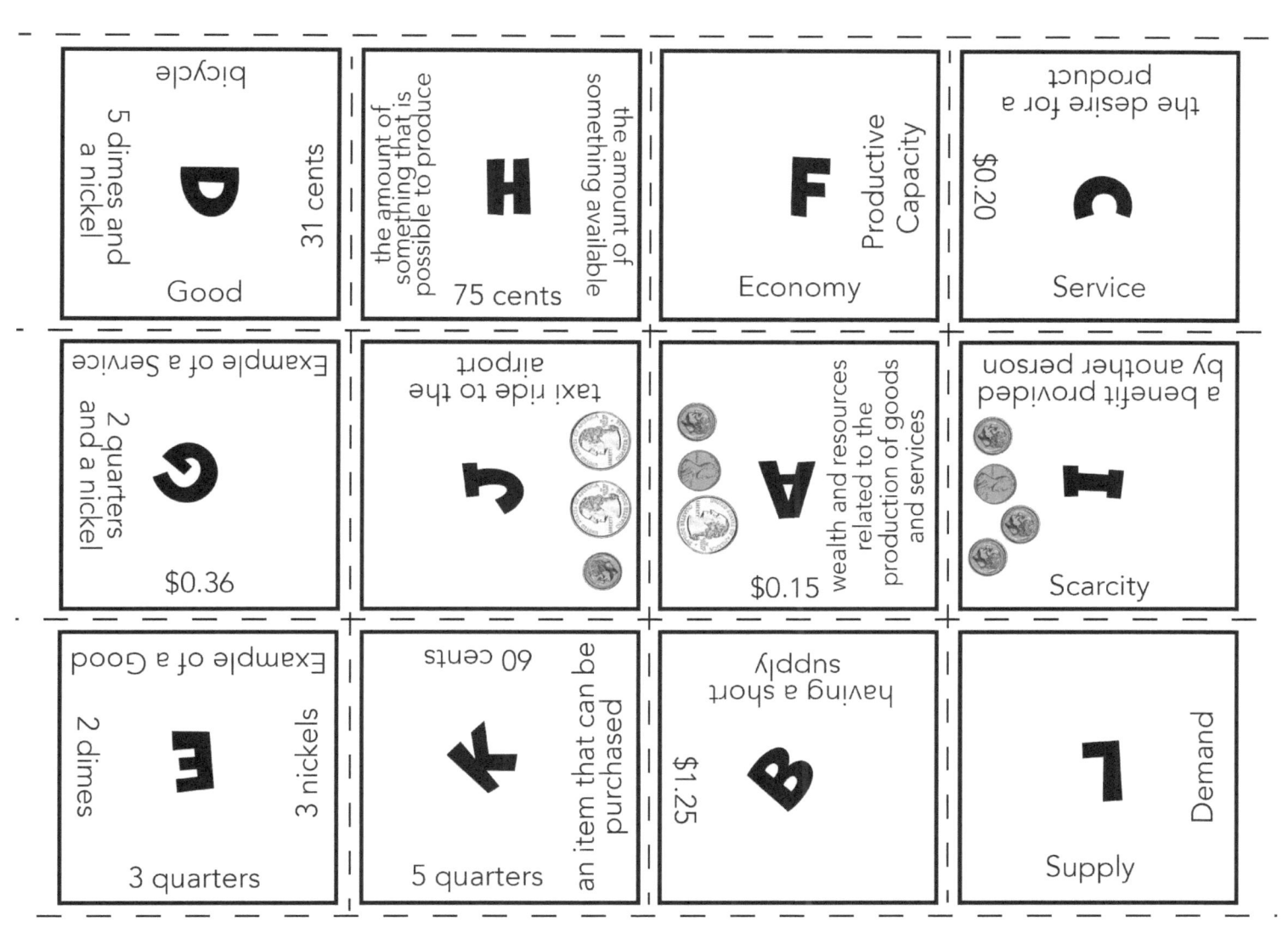

---

bicycle / **D** / 31 cents — 5 dimes and a nickel / Good	the amount of something that is possible to produce / **H** / 75 cents — the amount of something available	**F** / Economy — Productive Capacity	the desire for a product / **C** / $0.20 — Service
Example of a Service / **G** / $0.36 — 2 quarters and a nickel	taxi ride to the airport / **J** / $0.15 — (coins)	wealth and resources related to the production of goods and services / **A** / (coins)	a benefit provided by another person / **I** / (coins) — Scarcity
Example of a Good / **E** / 3 quarters — 2 dimes, 3 nickels	60 cents / **K** / 5 quarters — an item that can be purchased	having a short supply / **B** / $1.25 — Supply	**L** / Demand

---

CODE

To unlock the code, write the letters you see.
Left to right, and top to bottom is key.

MB Creations

Answer Keys

1 - Where in the World?

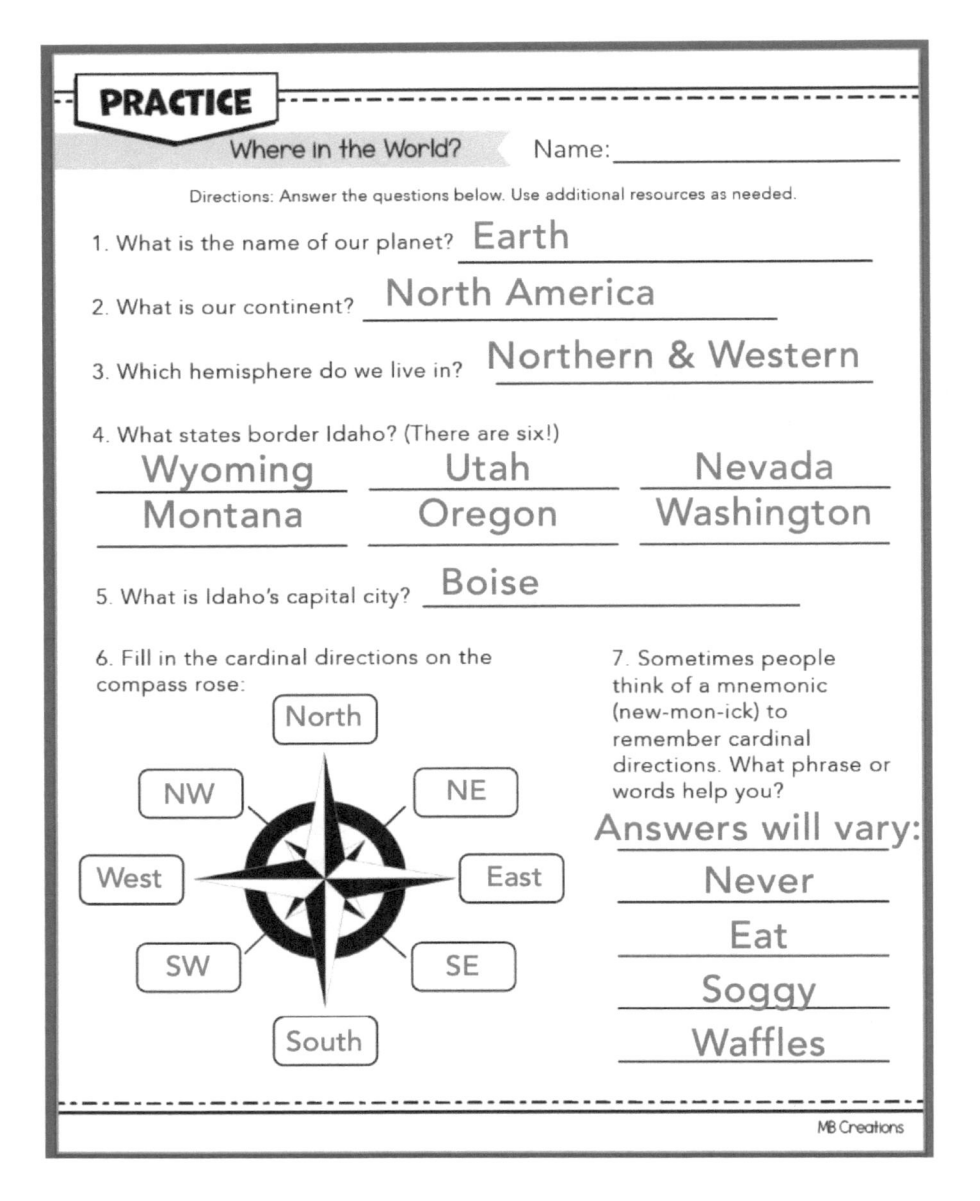

PRACTICE

Where in the World? Name: _____

Directions: Answer the questions below. Use additional resources as needed.

1. What is the name of our planet? __Earth__

2. What is our continent? __North America__

3. Which hemisphere do we live in? __Northern & Western__

4. What states border Idaho? (There are six!)
   __Wyoming__   __Utah__   __Nevada__
   __Montana__   __Oregon__   __Washington__

5. What is Idaho's capital city? __Boise__

6. Fill in the cardinal directions on the compass rose:
   - North
   - NW
   - NE
   - West
   - East
   - SW
   - SE
   - South

7. Sometimes people think of a mnemonic (new-mon-ick) to remember cardinal directions. What phrase or words help you?

   Answers will vary:
   __Never__
   __Eat__
   __Soggy__
   __Waffles__

MB Creations

> ASSESSMENT

Column 1:   Column 2:
H   B
J   E
F   G
A   K
I   D
L   C

PRACTICE #2

Answers will vary based on categories.

Possible Solution:

Continents
Asia
Australia

Oceans
Atlantic
Arctic
Pacific
Southern

Countries
Canada
China
Brazil
France

States
Idaho
Florida
Texas

MB Creations

1 - Where in the World?

>> ASSESSMENT

A - North America
B - Arctic Ocean
C - Europe
D - Asia
E - Atlantic Ocean
F - Pacific Ocean
G - Africa
H - South America
I - Indian Ocean
J - Australia
K - Southern Ocean
L - Antarctica

MYSTERY

Name:_____

Directions: Unscramble the letters to form words. Use the letters to discover the secret code below.

s e b i o
f p c i a c i
l y i t a
s h e h r e i m p e
o i h d a
t a n c r a a c t i
m o g i w n y
g n a t s o i h w n
h e r a t

B O I S E
★

P A C I F I C
☀

I T A L Y
▲

H E M I S P H E R E
●

I D A H O
●

A N T A R C T I C A
♥

W Y O M I N G
◆

W A S H I N G T O N
⬟

E A R T H
■

CODE

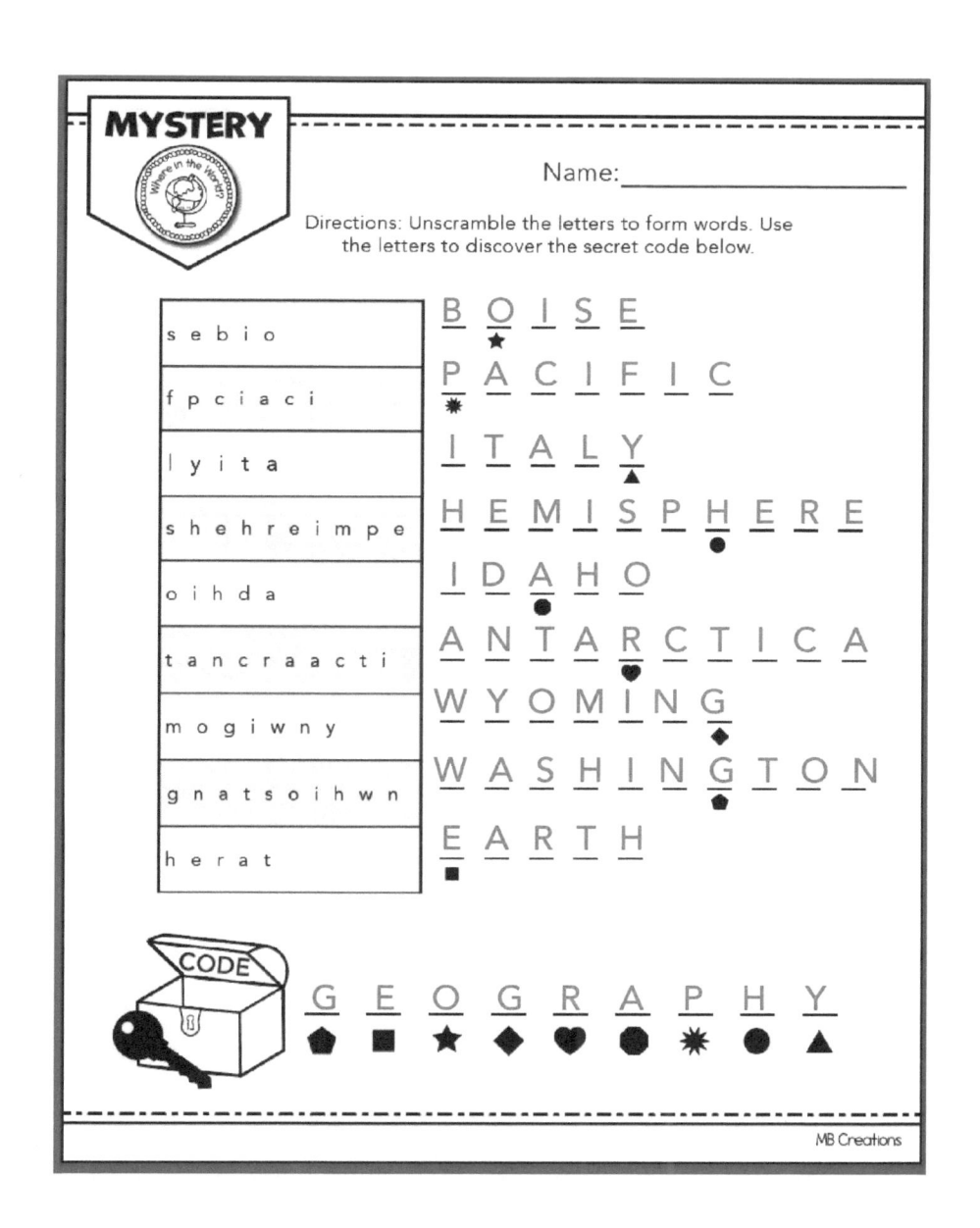

G E O G R A P H Y
⬟ ■ ★ ◆ ♥ ● ☀ ⬡ ▲

2 - All About Idaho

PRACTICE

All About Idaho   Name: _____

Directions: Use the readings and additional resources to answer the questions below.

1. Label each region. Then, list one city found in each region.

Answers will vary.

	Region:	City:
1	North	Kellogg
2	North Central	Lewiston
3	Southwest	Meridian
4	Central	Salmon
5	South Central	Burley
6	Eastern	Rexburg
7	Southeastern	Pocatello

2. Use a map and/or the internet to match each of the following places to a region. (Not all regions will be used).

- Craters of the Moon
- Yellowstone National Park
- Potato Capital
- Lake Coeur d'Alene
- Boise Capitol Building

- North
- North Central
- Southwest
- Central
- South Central
- Eastern
- Southeast

MB Creations

2 - All About Idaho

ASSESSMENT

> All About Idaho

Name:_____

Directions: Cut on the dashed lines and match the clues to each region of Idaho.

North
- Touches Canada
- Has lakes, forests, and mountains

North Central
- Home to Idaho's first capital (before it changed)
- Has rolling hills and prairies

Southwest
- Home to Idaho's current capital city
- Has mountains, deserts, and valleys

Central
- Popular place for tourists to ski, camp, and fish
- Major cities are Salmon & Stanley

Eastern
- Includes a small part of Yellowstone National Park

South Central
- Craters of the Moon
- Shoshone Falls

Southeast
- Potato capital of the world
- Has Lava Hot Springs

MB Creations

>> **ASSESSMENT** Answers will vary. Students who provide more details about landforms and cities have a deeper understanding of Idaho's geography.

MB Creations

2 - All About Idaho

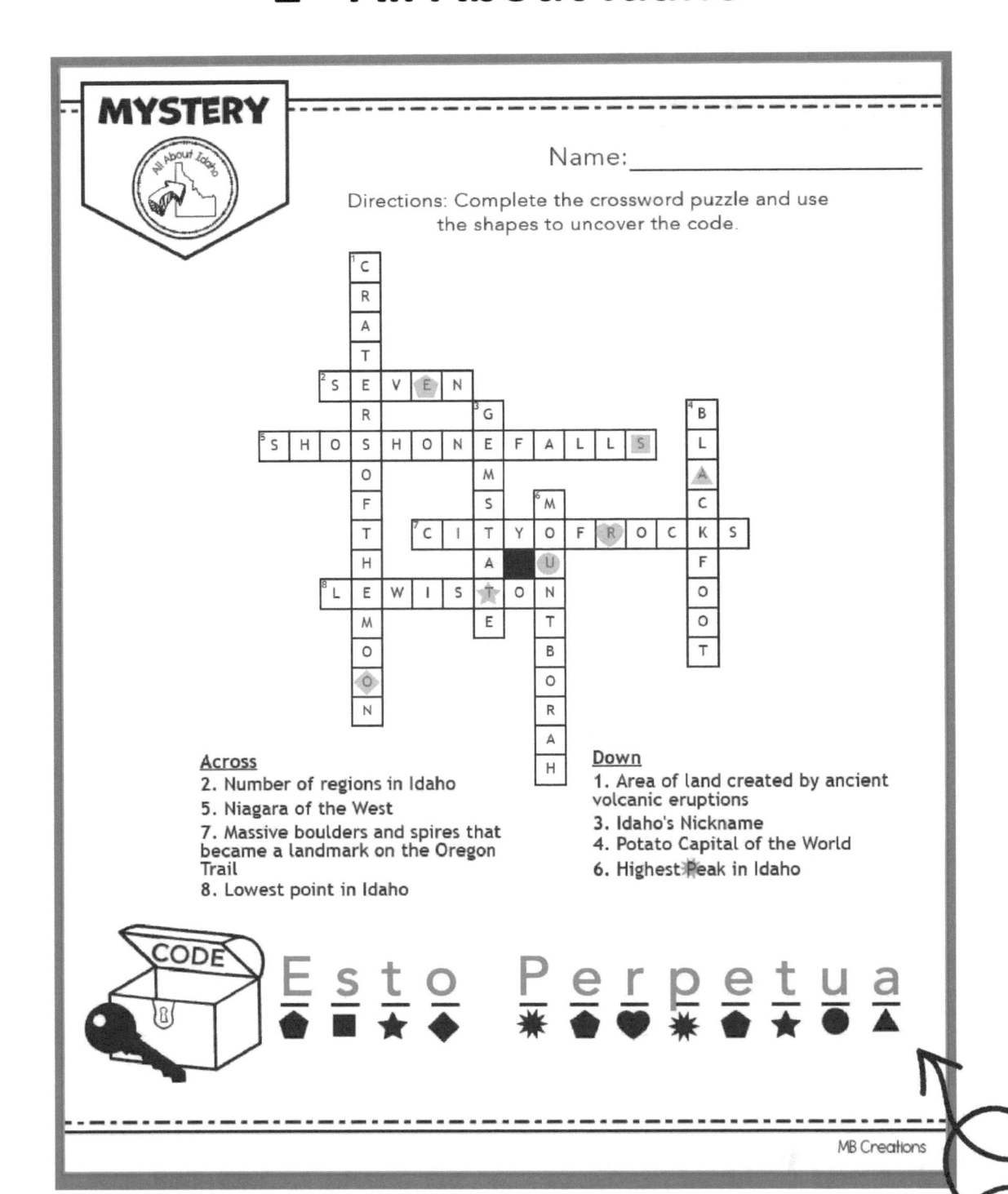

MYSTERY

Name: _____

Directions: Complete the crossword puzzle and use the shapes to uncover the code.

```
    1C
    R
    A
    T
  2S E V E N
    R       3G           4B
  5S H O S H O N E F A L L S
    O       M           A
    F       S     6M    C
    T     7C I T Y O F R O C K S
    H       A     U     F
  8L E W I S T O N     O
    M       N     T     O
    O       E     B     T
    O             O
    N             R
                  A
                  H
```

Across
2. Number of regions in Idaho
5. Niagara of the West
7. Massive boulders and spires that became a landmark on the Oregon Trail
8. Lowest point in Idaho

Down
1. Area of land created by ancient volcanic eruptions
3. Idaho's Nickname
4. Potato Capital of the World
6. Highest Peak in Idaho

CODE

E s t o   P e r p e t u a

State Motto - Means "Be eternal" or "It is perpetual."
It was chosen as a way to say, "Let Idaho live forever!"

MB Creations

3 - Idaho Symbols

PRACTICE

```
. . . . . . . . S A L A M A N D E R .
H U C K L E B E R R Y . . . . . . .
W H A G E R M A N H O R S E . . S .
H M . S P E R E G R I N E . . . Y .
I O . Q . . . . . . . . . . . . R .
T N . U . . . B L U E B I R D . I .
E A . A . . . . . . . . . . . . N .
P R . R T R O U T . . . . . . . G .
I C . E . . . . . . . . . . . . A .
N H . . . . . . . . . . . . . . . .
E . S T A R G A R N E T . . . . . .
. . . . . . A P P A L O O S A . . .
```

3 - Idaho Symbols

ASSESSMENT

> Idaho Symbols

Name:_____

Directions: Fill in as many Idaho symbols on the bingo board below. Can you get...

☐ three across? ☐ four down? ☐ all four corners? ☐ the entire board?

Flower: Syringa	Bird: Mountain Bluebird	Gem: Idaho Star Garnet
Amphibian: Giant Salamander	Fossil: Hagerman Horse	Raptor: Peregrine Falcon
Horse: Appaloosa	Fruit: Huckleberry	Tree: Western White Pine
Dance: Square Dance	Fish: Cutthroat Trout	Insect: Monarch Butterfly

MB Creations

>> **ASSESSMENT** Answers will vary; students show more advanced analyzing skills when they are able to support their chosen symbol with multiple reasons.

MB Creations

3 - Idaho Symbols

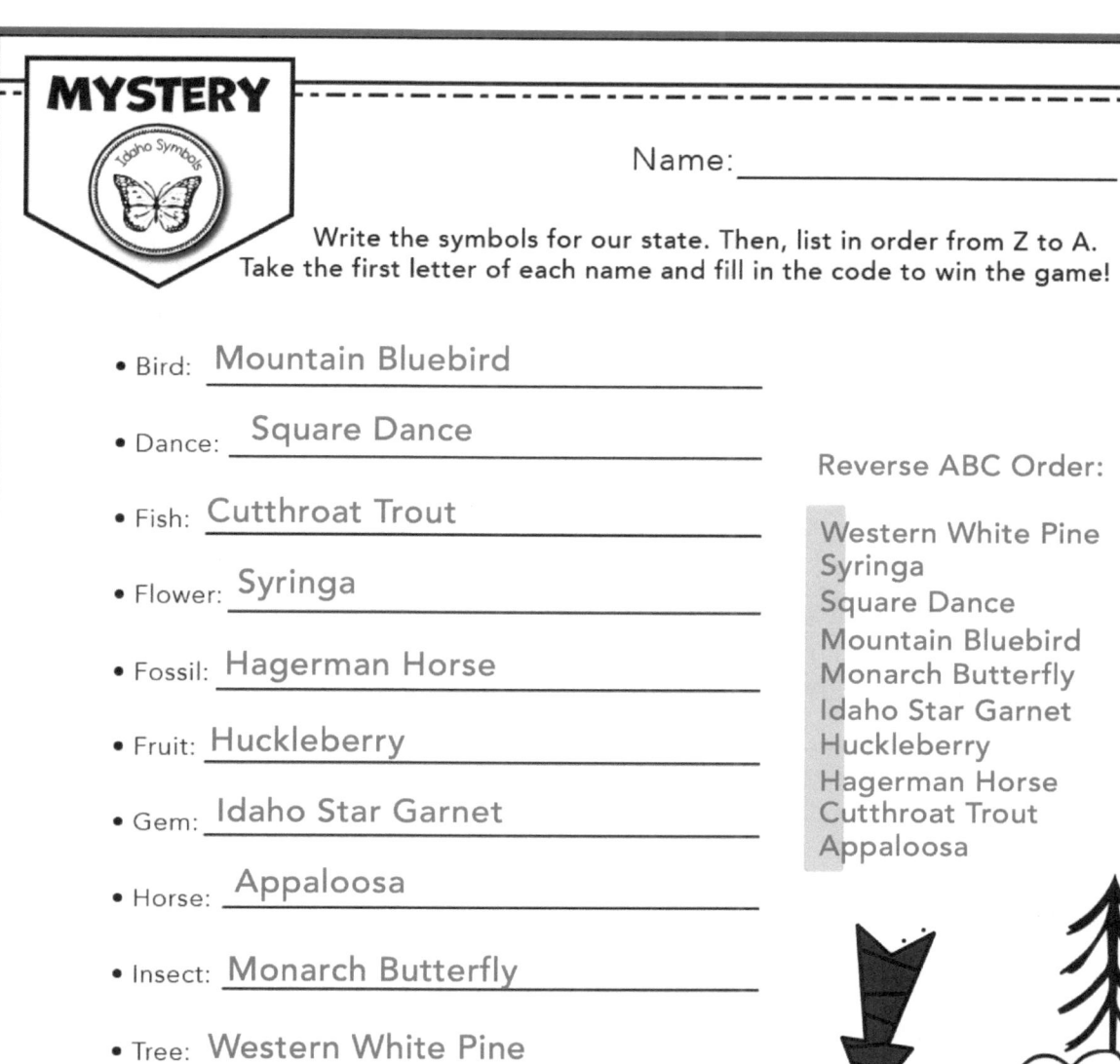

MYSTERY — Idaho Symbols

Name: _____

Write the symbols for our state. Then, list in order from Z to A. Take the first letter of each name and fill in the code to win the game!

- Bird: **Mountain Bluebird**
- Dance: **Square Dance**
- Fish: **Cutthroat Trout**
- Flower: **Syringa**
- Fossil: **Hagerman Horse**
- Fruit: **Huckleberry**
- Gem: **Idaho Star Garnet**
- Horse: **Appaloosa**
- Insect: **Monarch Butterfly**
- Tree: **Western White Pine**

Reverse ABC Order:

Western White Pine
Syringa
Square Dance
Mountain Bluebird
Monarch Butterfly
Idaho Star Garnet
Huckleberry
Hagerman Horse
Cutthroat Trout
Appaloosa

CODE: W S S M M I H H C A

MB Creations

4 - Idaho Counties

PRACTICE #1

_O_ Benewah
_F_ Bonneville
_M_ Butte
_A_ Caribou
_J_ Ellmore
_D_ Franklin
_L_ Fremont

_E_ Lemhi
_I_ Lewis
_G_ Lincoln
_B_ Nez Perce
_N_ Payette
_C_ Power
_H_ Twin Falls
_K_ Valley

> ASSESSMENT

- Answers will vary; Students can color draw an arrow to label on the map.
- 4 = D and 5 = B

MYSTERY

Find the dot that's out of place.
Write it's name and win the race!

Garfield

MB Creations

4 - Idaho Counties

ASSESSMENT

ASSESSMENT
>> Idaho's Counties

Name: _____

Directions: Use knowledge from your research to answer the questions below.

COUNTY TRIVIA!

1. Which of the following counties was the first to be organized?

   A) Boise
   B) Owyhee ✓
   C) Gooding
   D) Lewis

2. How many counties were already part of the Idaho Territory when Idaho became a state in 1890?

   A) 18 ✓
   B) 44
   C) 3
   D) 28

3. What is Idaho's largest county by size (square miles)?

   A) Camas
   B) Elmore
   C) Bingham
   D) Idaho ✓

4. What is Idaho's smallest county by size (square miles)?

   A) Payette ✓
   B) Cassia
   C) Teton
   D) Washington

5. What is Idaho's most populated county?

   A) Gem
   B) Ada ✓
   C) Kootenai
   D) Boundary

6. What is Idaho's least populated county?

   A) Madison
   B) Lincoln
   C) Power
   D) Clark ✓

7. In which county is the capital city located?

   A) Canyon
   B) Jerome
   C) Boise
   D) Ada ✓

MB Creations

5 – Famous Idahoans

> ASSESSMENT

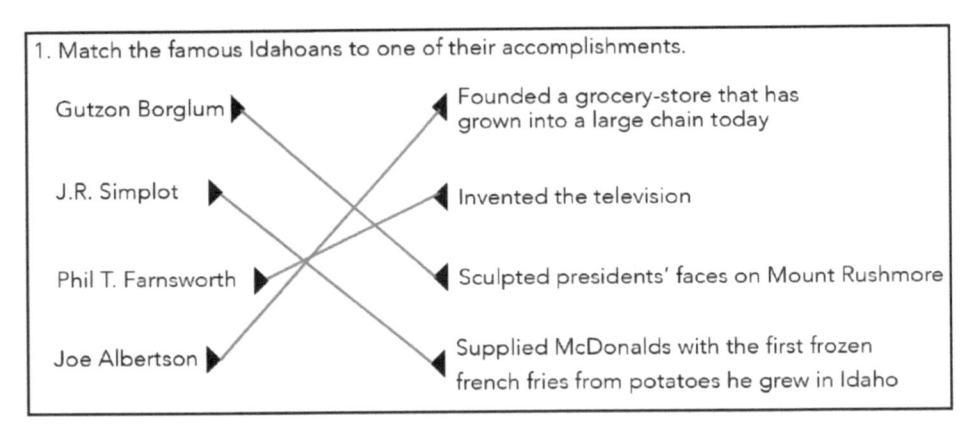

1. Match the famous Idahoans to one of their accomplishments.

- Gutzon Borglum → Sculpted presidents' faces on Mount Rushmore
- J.R. Simplot → Supplied McDonalds with the first frozen french fries from potatoes he grew in Idaho
- Phil T. Farnsworth → Invented the television
- Joe Albertson → Founded a grocery-store that has grown into a large chain today

2. Answers will vary; Students who are able to write about a person they did not study for their own "Who Am I?" project demonstrate the ability to remember details from peers' projects and/or supplemental readings.

>> ASSESSMENT

Answers will vary; below are ideas of possible perspectives. Students should be able to form reasonable perspectives based on their knowledge of the individuals.

Chief Joseph:
1 - Against the Iron Horse because it would destroy his homeland and food sources
2 - Favorable because he supported equal rights for all
3 - Against because the United States did not protect his people so he may feel unwilling to serve them in battle

Elias Pierce:
1 - Favorable because he could transport gold and supplies more easily
2 - Favorable because he was focused on building a mining empire and could see the value women added to mining towns through various jobs
3 - Favorable because he had a history of serving in the United States military

Statira Robinson:
1 - Favorable because she had a difficult journey traveling from Ohio to Idaho in her life
2 - Favorable because she was a woman (Idaho's first school teacher)
3 - Favorable because her husband served in the military

Joe Albertson:
1 - Favorable; though before his time, Albertson created a large grocery chain and would have benefited from the railroad in the 1800s had his stores been in operation
2 - Favorable because he was known for philanthropy and likely wanted equal rights for all
3 - Favorable because he supported drives to collect metal for the war effort and sponsored war bonds

MB Creations

5 – Famous Idahoans

MYSTERY

Name: _____

Directions: Decipher the rebus puzzles below by writing the first and last names of people who impacted Idaho. Then, use one of the names to decipher the code.

🔵p=w+🐑r=i 🌊-ve+🔔-be+a+🍚-ri	j+👟-sh a+💡-bu+e+🎯-da+☀u=o
William Wallace	Joe Albertson

⬆-u+🎩-at+i+🔒-ck 🚗c=f+🗽y=s🐺-lf+🎯-da+h	c+👔t=h+f 🌹r=j+⬆-u+h
Philo Farnsworth	Chief Joseph

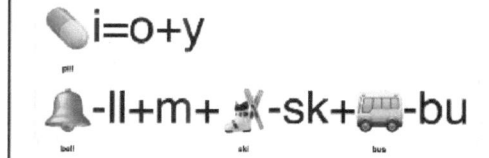

j+🐑-am 📼-vh+i+👨-an+🔌-ug+🐂x=t	🔵i=o+y 🔔-ll+m+🎿-sk+🚌-bu
JR Simplot	Polly Bemis

To unlock the code, focus only on the last
Fill in the letters and try to work fast.

A l b e r t s o n
_ _ _ _ _ _ _ _ _

MB Creations

6 - Government

PRACTICE

Government   Name:_____

Directions: Use your knowledge and information from the reading to answer the questions below.

1. Write the name of each type of government in order of rank and power. Which government is at the top (and has overarching rule)?

Pyramid:
- National
- State | Tribal
- County | City

2. What are the three branches of national government? List one power of each branch. (What do they do?)

1. **Legislative**
- Makes laws; House of Representatives Senate

2. **Executive**
- Carries out laws; run by President of the United States

3. **Judicial**
- Enforces laws; court system

3. Why is our government organized into three different branches? The government can divide responsibilities and power amongst three branches so no group gains too much control. This is a system of checks and balances.

MB Creations

6 - Government

ASSESSMENT
Government

Name:_____

1. Who runs each branch of government at the national level in the United States?

Legislative Branch:	Executive Branch:	Judicial Branch:
Congress (Senate & House of Representatives)	President	Chief Justice of the Supreme Court (Judges)

2. True or False...

__F__ A tribal government overrules the federal government.

__T__ State and city governments utilize a system of checks and balances by dividing up responsbilities similar to the federal government.

__F__ The executive branch makes laws for the people based on the Constitution.

__F__ The president decides how many senators from each state can join Congress.

__T__ The legislative branch taxes the people and manages government funds.

3. If you were to write a constitution for your school or classroom, what rights and laws would you include? Why?

Answers will vary; students should be able to describe rights that are important to students and laws that will help everyone stay safe and access their rights.
_____
_____
_____

MB Creations

6 - Government

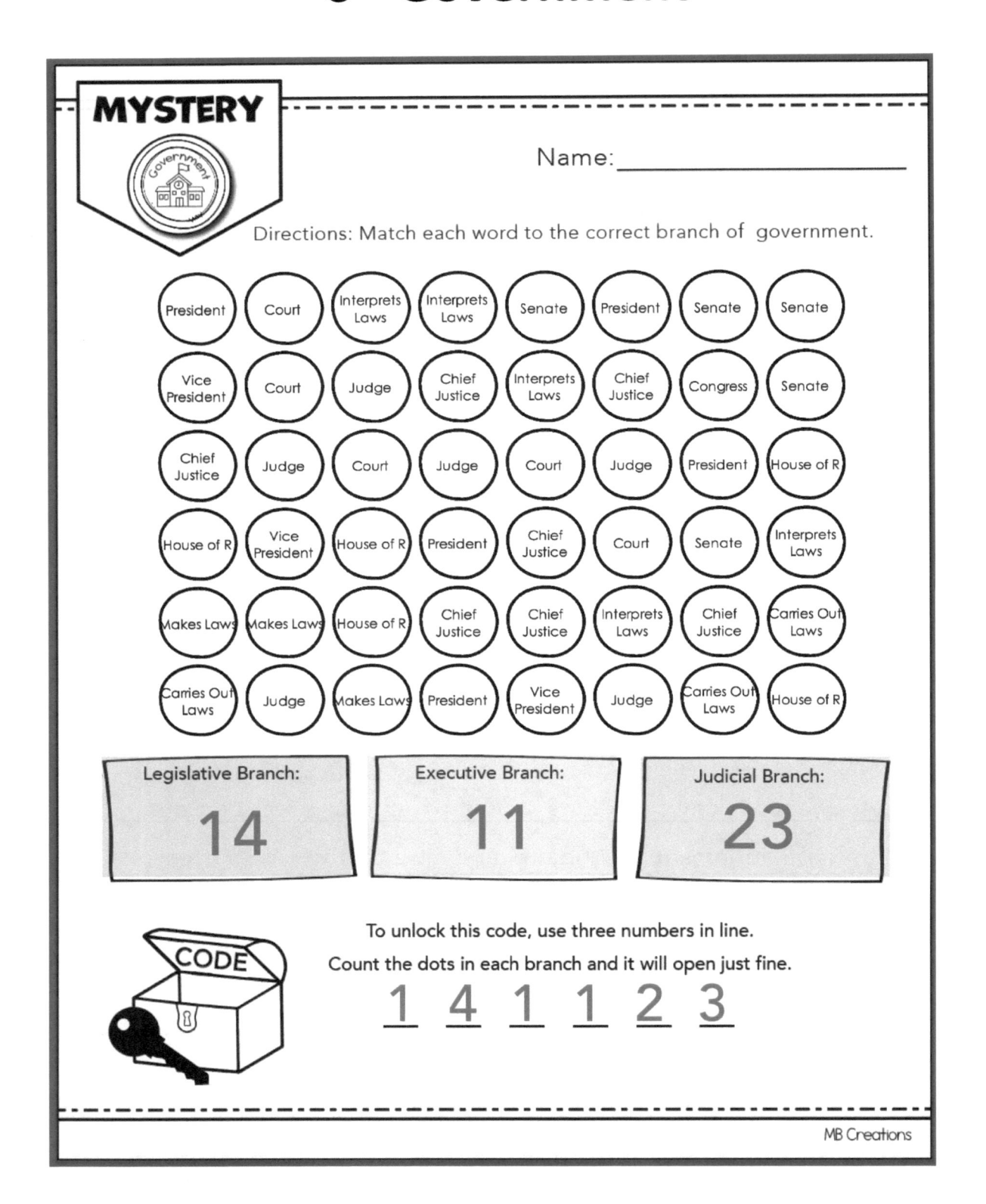

MYSTERY

Name: _____

Directions: Match each word to the correct branch of government.

President	Court	Interprets Laws	Interprets Laws	Senate	President	Senate	Senate
Vice President	Court	Judge	Chief Justice	Interprets Laws	Chief Justice	Congress	Senate
Chief Justice	Judge	Court	Judge	Court	Judge	President	House of R
House of R	Vice President	House of R	President	Chief Justice	Court	Senate	Interprets Laws
Makes Laws	Makes Laws	House of R	Chief Justice	Chief Justice	Interprets Laws	Chief Justice	Carries Out Laws
Carries Out Laws	Judge	Makes Laws	President	Vice President	Judge	Carries Out Laws	House of R

Legislative Branch: 14

Executive Branch: 11

Judicial Branch: 23

To unlock this code, use three numbers in line.
Count the dots in each branch and it will open just fine.

<u>1</u> <u>4</u> <u>1</u> <u>1</u> <u>2</u> <u>3</u>

MB Creations

7 - Economics

» Assessment answers will vary. Review student responses to see how deep of an understanding they have about the topics covered in this lesson.

MYSTERY

Name: _____

Directions: Cut apart the puzzle pieces. Connect the matching sides.

F Productive Capacity / Economy	**H** the amount of something that is possible to produce / 75 cents	**L** the amount of something available / Demand
A wealth and resources related to the production of goods and services / $0.15 / 3 nickels	**E** 3 quarters / 2 dimes / Example of a Good	**C** the desire for a product / $0.20 / Service
G $0.36 / 2 quarters and a nickel / Example of a Service	**D** bicycle / 5 dimes and a nickel / Good	**I** a benefit provided by another person / 31 cents / Scarcity
J taxi ride to the airport / 60 cents	**K** an item that can be purchased / 5 quarters	**B** having a short supply / $1.25

CODE: F H L A E C G D I J K B

To unlock the code, write the letters you see.
Left to right, and top to bottom is key.

MB Creations

FIND MORE FAVORITES

Visit **mbcreations.net** to find more teaching and learning resources.

#mbcreations4education

MEET THE AUTHOR

Megan Bell Smith has a BS in Early Childhood/Special Education, an MA in Elementary Education + Gifted Endorsement, and an EDS in Instructional Design and Online Learning. She has taught special education, preschool, fourth grade, and gifted and talented classes.

Made in United States
Troutdale, OR
04/10/2025